Contemplating
YOUR BELLYBUTTON

Written by Jun Nanao
Illustrated by Tomoko Hasegawa

Translated by Amanda Mayer Stinchecum

A CURIOUS NELL BOOK

 Kane/Miller Book Publishers

Brooklyn, New York & La Jolla, California

What's that?
A bellybutton
that sticks out?

Whenever Tettchan looks at his bellybutton, he thinks, "Everyone laughs at a bellybutton that sticks out. Why do I need a bellybutton, anyway?

Ha, ha—a bellybutton that sticks out!

Oh, my, I have a bellybutton that sticks out too!

It's nothing to be ashamed of.
Everyone has a funny-looking bellybutton.

You shouldn't play with your bellybutton,
Tettchan, just because you think it doesn't
have any use.

Before you were born, your bellybutton was
very important.

He's playing with his
bellybutton again . . .

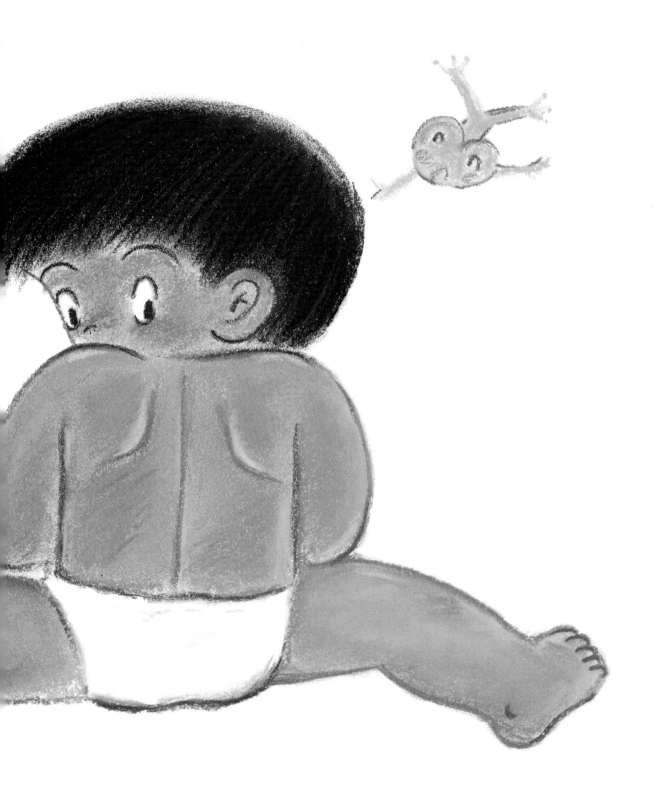

A single cord?

You know, Tettchan, while you were still in your mother's belly, your body was connected to her body by a single cord.

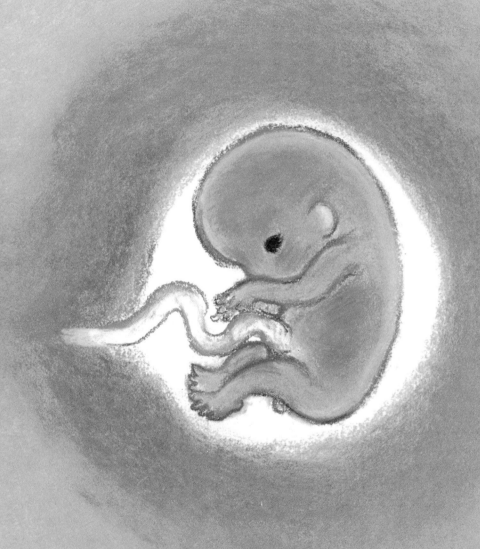

This cord brought food from your mother's body to you,

and you gradually grew.

Without eating anything at all,
you very soon got bigger and bigger.

Ah—! The baby moved in my belly!

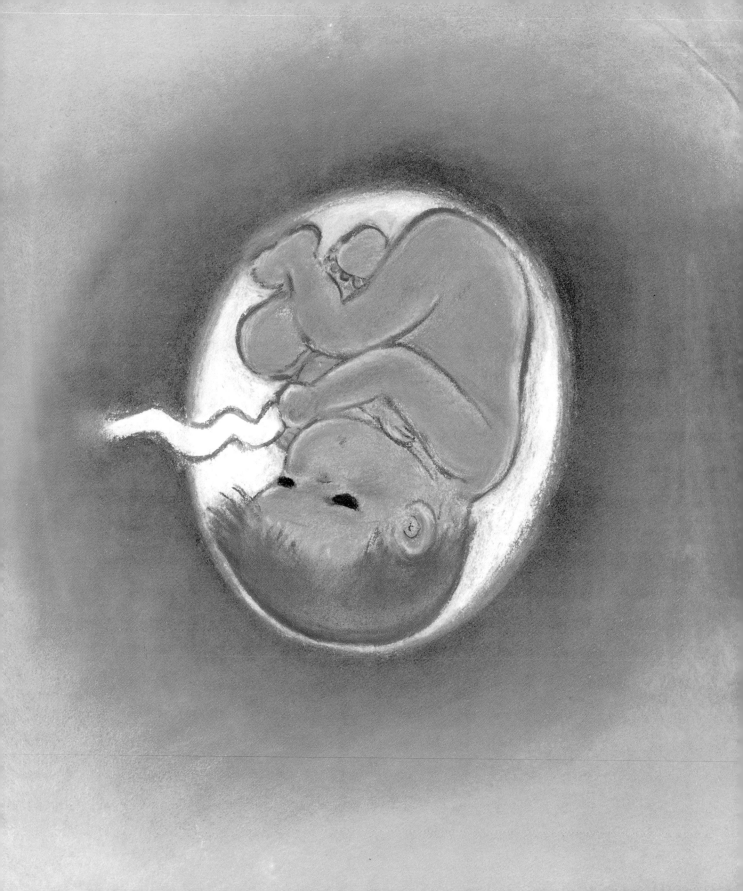

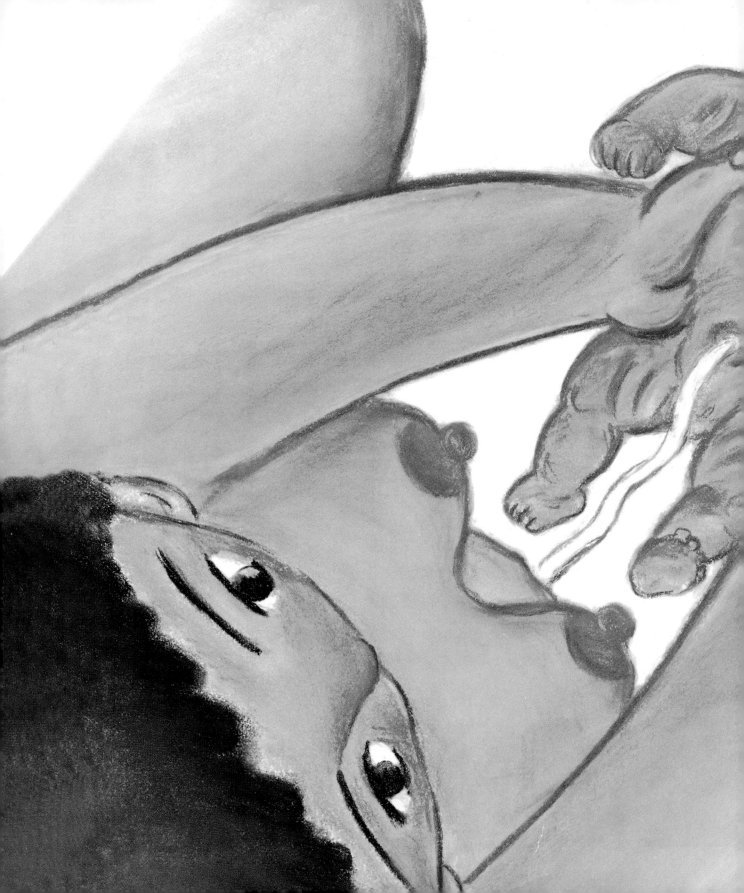

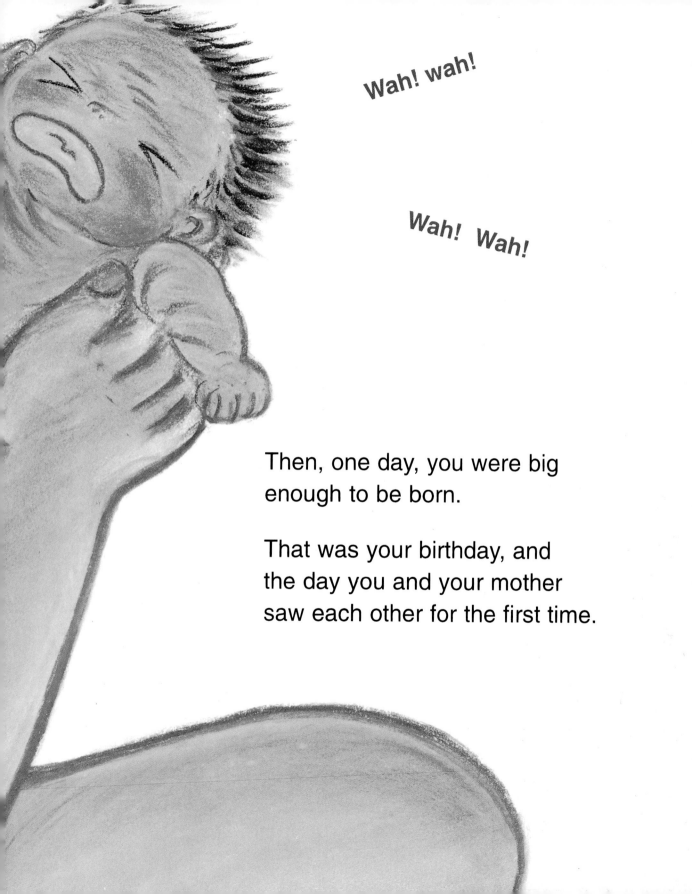

Wah! wah!

Wah! Wah!

Then, one day, you were big
enough to be born.

That was your birthday, and
the day you and your mother
saw each other for the first time.

The doctor cut the cord with a
special pair of scissors. Snip!

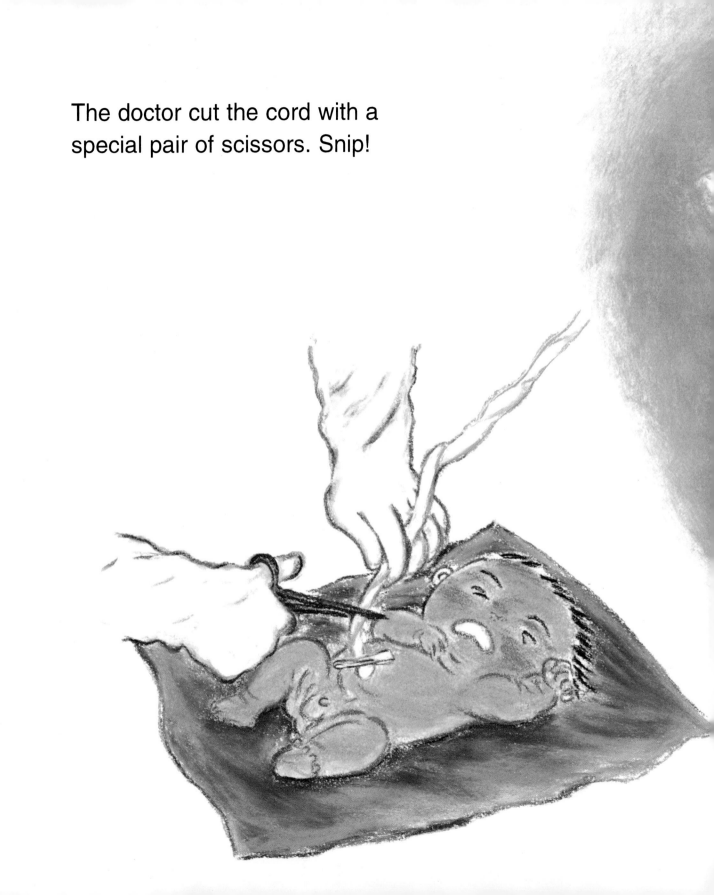

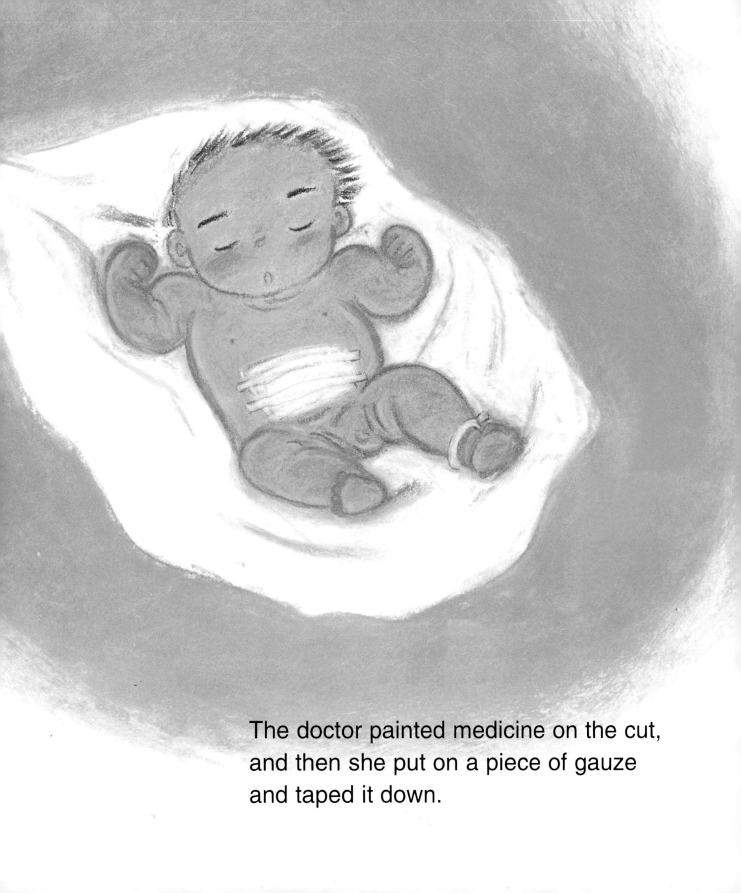

The doctor painted medicine on the cut,
and then she put on a piece of gauze
and taped it down.

Even though the cord was cut,
it was all right.

Now you sucked milk from your
mother's breast and grew bigger.

Days went by.

The end of the cord healed and dropped off—plop.

What was left after it fell off is your bellybutton, Tettchan.

Your bellybutton is an important mark of your birth from your mother.

Your father's bellybutton is a mark of your father's birth from *his* mother.

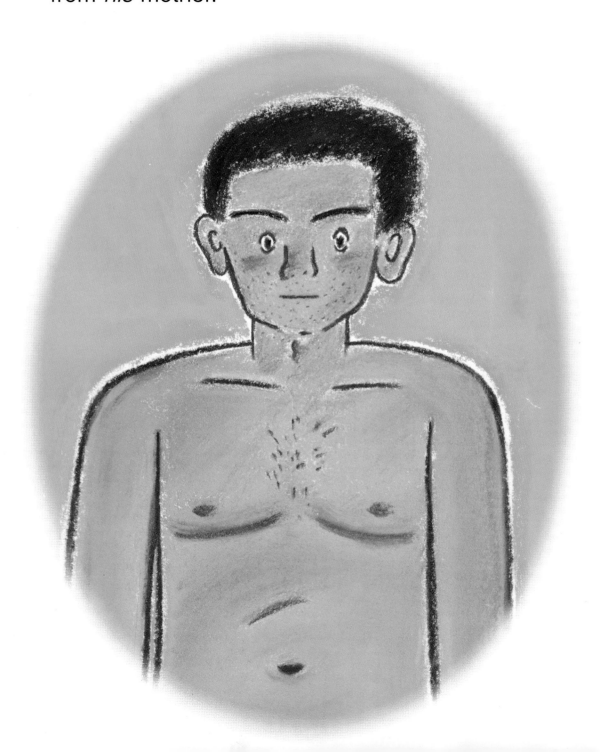

Your mother's bellybutton is a mark of her birth from *her* mother.

It's not always easy to keep your bellybutton clean.

The wrinkles can become the home for germs.

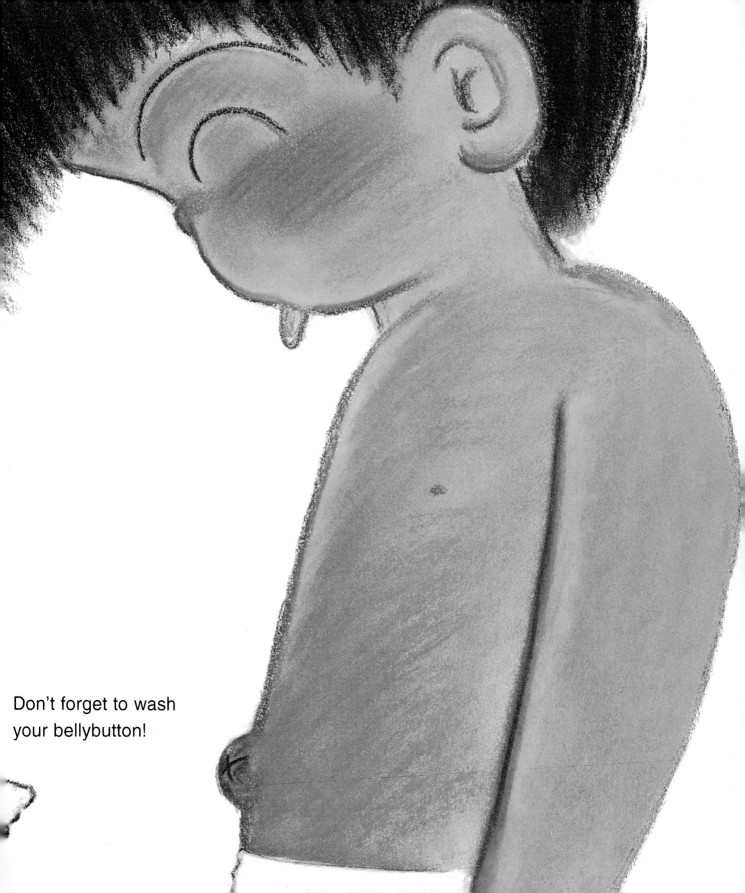

Don't forget to wash
your bellybutton!

When you get out of the bathtub,
be sure to dry your bellybutton
with a towel.

Now cover up . . . sleep well . . . sweet dreams.

First American Edition 1995 by Kane/Miller Book Publishers
Brooklyn, New York & La Jolla, California

Originally published in Japan in 1985 under the title *Oheso Ni Kiite Goran*
Text by Jun Nanao, illustrations by Tomoko Hasegawa
Copyright © 1985 by Jun Nanao and Tomoko Hasegawa
English translation rights arranged with *Akane Shobo Co., Ltd.*
through Japan Foreign-Rights Centre.

American text copyright © 1995 Kane/Miller Book Publishers

Library of Congress Catalog Card Number 95-77134
ISBN 0-916291-60-X

Printed and bound in Singapore by Tien Wah Press Pte. Ltd.
2 3 4 5 6 7 8 9 10

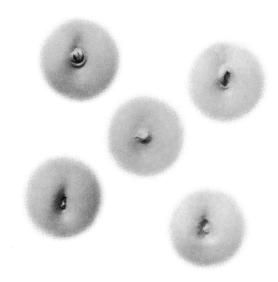

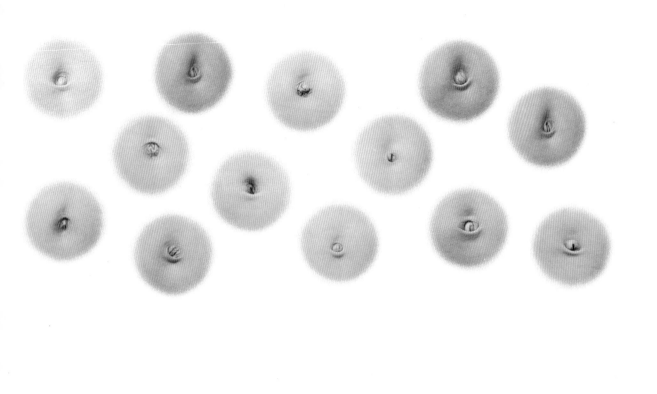